Unlock Your Greatness

8 Ways to be Successful in High School and Beyond

Isaiah Swift

Acknowledgments

I would like to thank God for His many blessings. I would also like to thank my parents for their continuous support and I want my entire family to know that I love and appreciate them. Also, I want to acknowledge those of you who have taken the time to make the investment and purchase this book. I want to share this moment with you. I wish that those of you holding this book could experience this feeling of excitement that I have. It is indescribable. Many of you are students, parents, educators, principals, mentors, entrepreneurs. I'm not sure if you even know me or not, which isn't even a factor. I'm just glad that you have this book, and I want to say thank you from the bottom of my heart for coming on this journey with me.

Dedication

Dedicated to my mother for helping me make important
decisions and inspiring me by the way she lives her life.

Table of Contents

Introduction 1

Chapter 1: Don't Be Afraid to Ask for Help 6

Chapter 2: Be the Change You Want to see 13

Chapter 3: Stay Ahead of the Game 19

Chapter 4: Go the Extra Mile 31

Chapter 5: Make it Count 39

Chapter 6: Never Give Up 47

Chapter 7: Understand the Importance of Financial Education 59

Chapter 8: Take Advantage of Scholarships and Grants 67

Chapter 9: It's all Worth it 75

Introduction

On this early morning, I'm sitting in the corner of a coffee shop by myself, and it feels so good to be doing this right now. I'm beginning a journey in my life that I would have never dreamt of in a million years. I'm a sophomore at Norfolk State University, majoring in business with a concentration in finance. Recently, I had a great conversation with one of the best people on the planet, Matt Maddix, who is the founder of Maddix Publishing and also the father to Caleb Maddix, co-founder. I came across an ad on Facebook that was promoting their publishing company, and I thought I'd sign up to schedule a strategy call with Matt regarding the process of writing a book. Matt and I set up a call a couple weeks later, and we discussed the process of going through his publishing company so that I could write a book. At first, I was a little timid, and I told Matt that I thought it would take me a year to write the book. He assured me that the process would be much sooner than that. As a young black male that has faced different challenges and pressures as a teen, and I come from a household where I didn't have a lot of money.

However, when I graduated high school, I was able to go to college on a full ride scholarship. That night, Matt told me "Isaiah you have such a great story, why don't you use it to help students in high school?" I reflected upon that suggestion for a few hours and later that evening, I called Matt and informed him that I was going to make the decision and join Maddix Publishing. I have had my fair share of life experiences but for the most part, I haven't been through much. I just turned 20 years old, and my time of this earth has been fairly short. I used to think that in order to write a book or do something great, you needed to be around 30 or 40 years old.

But that is too long for me. I'm ready to be a part of a generation that's not waiting to serve, not waiting to inspire, and not waiting to make a difference in the lives of others. Rather, I'm a part of a generation that is ready to utilize what they have instead of focusing on their limitations.

This moment for me is surreal because I would have never imagined that I would have the opportunity to help people just like me on such a massive level. In my opinion, writing a book is such a high accomplishment, and it's not often that you find too many college students taking on this type of task. Keep in mind, I am a sophomore, which means I am midway through college and need to ensure that I stay on track. This meant that I had to manage my time well while still staying focused on my goals.

I want to share with you why I decided to write this book. I had such a great time in high school, not in the sense of going to a lot of parties, being wild or skipping class, but in regards to some of the decisions that I made. I'm not that old, but looking back, there aren't too many decisions that I regret making in high school. I had a great relationship with my teachers and guidance counselor, and I took advantage of almost every opportunity I was offered while I was in high school. I don't know all things, but one thing I do know is that it doesn't take a rocket scientist to be able to give advice on how to be successful in high school.

Even if you are a high school dropout, I'm sure you have at least been to the 5th grade. Someone who finished the 5th grade can give advice to someone in the third grade or fourth grade. Now replace your success in the fifth grade with something that you've previously accomplished. Maybe you led a volunteer project in your community, saved money from your job, or you go to the gym on a weekly basis. The point I'm trying to convey is that you can use your experiences to help somebody else.

I could easily write a book telling you all the things that I accomplished in high school, but that would just leave you with inspiration. Not only do I want to inspire, but I also want to give you practical tools so that you can do the same. My goal is to show you eight steps for becoming successful in high school and beyond so that you can replicate and apply them. The way you apply these eight steps might be different than the way that I executed them, but that's the unique thing about it. We all are designed differently. I'm successful, not because of money, materialism or status. I'm successful because I said it, I believe it - the end. If you're reading this right now, I want you to know that there is something great on the inside of you. I'm not asking you; I'm telling you. If you didn't have anything great on the inside of you, then you wouldn't be here. So, stop trying to compare your life to others. We are all extraordinary.

My favorite pair of shoes are my leather brown Sperry's. They fit my feet because I wear my size, which is a size 9, and I look dapper in them. I bet we all can agree that Sperry's are a great pair of quality shoes. But if I tried to wear a size 11, it would be uncomfortable. Why? Because that's not my size. If I'm not wearing my size, then I'm doing myself a disservice because I'm not staying true to who I really am. You have to realize that I can provide you with the steps on how to be successful in high school and beyond, but you might not see the same results as I've seen. And that's okay if you don't. You will get the results that suit your journey.

It does my heart good to know that you at least applied yourself. When you apply yourself to an area, it means that you executed. You took one step forward instead of one step back. You walked into new territory, and you're ahead of those that chose to remain complacent. The goal of this book is to get you to be the change that you want to see. I'm sure you've heard that before, but did you really grasp it or was it just another quote that you liked on your Instagram feed and kept scrolling? The truth is, quotes won't work until you do.

Let's make this happen. High school is one of the best times in your life because in high school, you start to explore your true identity. Sometimes negativity from social media, peers and even family can cause you to spend hours questioning whether you are capable of achieving something. Because of this, it can become normal for you to constantly doubt yourself, underperform in your grades and isolate yourself from others based on their opinions.

One thing you must realize is that your current identity is not your permanent identity. Every day your identity is constantly changing because of yourself and other outside influences. I believe we are who we associate ourselves with. Also, one of the biggest factors that shape your identity is the person you see looking back at you in the mirror. Some of those moments are short, quick glimpses while some moments take longer. Regardless of how long it takes, we formulate our own opinions of who we are. Believe or not, you can use those moments to change the course of your entire life. In this book, I'm going to show you how you can apply yourself not just in high school, but beyond.

I'll admit that this has been a journey for me, but it was all worth it. I need you to "Unlock Your Greatness" and be the best version of yourself. In life, 10% is what happens to you and 90% is how you respond. I'm sure there are great books out there tailored towards high school students, but this book is different. This book isn't written by an adult who has been out of the high school environment for years. This book is written by a freshly graduated high school student that can identify with the current struggles and trends that are present in every high school across the United States. I am confident that this book will give you a fresh perspective on your high school experience and give you tools that will help you now and in the future.

Chapter 1
Don't Be Afraid to Ask for Help

"I never ask for help." ~ No Successful Person Ever

Before I dive into teaching you the steps to becoming successful in high school, I have to share a life-changing situation that occurred during my childhood. I believe that at times, life can be your greatest teacher. No matter what circumstance you go through, whether big or small, life's lessons can serve as some of the greatest teachers. When I was in fifth grade, my mom bought me my first bike. I was so happy to receive my bike because it meant something to me. It was almost like my car. On a hot summer's day, I would go outside, hop on my blue bike and push the pedals as fast as I could up and down the sidewalk.

As a 10-year-old, there was no better feeling than to be able to ride my bicycle with the wind blowing behind my back and the cool breeze going through my shirt. Pedaling up and down the sidewalk caused such as refreshing feeling. With one hand on the wheel, I would use the other hand to wave at my older neighbors as they sat across the street in their chairs and watched in amazement. On one particular day, I told myself, "You know what? I am a bike riding expert. Why don't I show my older neighbors how good I am and perform a few tricks for them?"

Everytime I rode my bike, the smiles on their faces would make me feel good, so I thought I would show them something that I thought they had never seen before. I was so eager and excited. I rushed out the door, grabbed my bike from the side patio of our one-story apartment and proceeded to hop on it and pedal away. Both of my older neighbors were sitting outside, and I said to myself, "Great! This is going to be the day that I impress them with my bicycle skills."

In my head I said, "Here we go! Bicycle trick number one." Again, with one hand on the handlebar, I used the other hand to wave at them. Immediately, they both smiled and waved back. I wanted them to know that only I could do that. Only I could ride my bicycle with one hand. Then, I went on to put both hands on the handlebar and pedaled as fast as I could all the way down to the stop sign at the end of our street. After I made it down there, I made a U-turn and began pedaling as fast as I could again. This time, the neighbors were on my right side, so I figured I should wave at them again. As I began to approach, I waved at them again, and they waved back, smiled and even sat up straight in their chairs just to see if I was still the same young man from two minutes earlier.

I thought, "OK, now that I have their attention, I'm going to do another trick." With my right hand in the air still waving at them, I raised my left hand in the air and the lifted both of my arms as high as I could off of the handlebar. These were the two most daring seconds of my life. In an attempt to impress my older neighbors across the street from me, I rode my bike with both hands raised in the air as I began to turn my face and smile at them in total amazement.

Suddenly, I remember glancing down, and before I could put both hands back on the handlebar, I lost my balance. My feet stopped pedaling, and my wheel made a sharp right turn, which caused me to fall. My face slammed to the ground. I was not wearing a helmet and luckily, I was not severely injured. However, I knew that my two and a half minutes of bicycling fame were over.

I laid on the ground for about another two minutes, slightly bruised. Moreover, I was shocked and embarrassed. Seconds later, I heard these words. "Get up! You'll be OK." And then, the other neighbor yelled, "You got this man. You're a big boy." To my disbelief, my shame and embarrassment quickly faded away. As I stood up, I didn't even bother to look at my older neighbors that were across the street. Although on the inside, it felt good knowing that they had just said some encouraging words to me. I picked up my bike and walked it back to my apartment.

You might be wondering, what exactly does me riding a bike and falling off it have to do with how to be successful in high school? Well, there are many times in life that you're going to make mistakes. You might find yourself striving towards a certain goal, like I was. I wanted to prove to my older neighbors how good I was on my bicycle, only to discover that I was not as good as I thought I was. It wasn't because I was incapable of riding a bike, but I lacked the required persistent practice to perform tricks. If you find yourself in a situation where you, "fall off your bike," you have to learn how to get up. Shake off the dust from the fall and keep it moving, whether you have people there to encourage you or not.

I could have stayed there on the ground and waited for help, but the reality is that there will be times when there will be no help in sight. Do not get me wrong, you have parents, teachers, mentors, guidance counselors and even good friends who will push you to greatness, but it's not up to them to make the decision for you. As a teenager, there are areas that you might excel in, whether it is good grades, athletic ability, singing, public speaking, art, dance and the list goes on. You might even practice every single day at getting better at some of these things. When you do practice, put forth effort, and try to improve your skills, don't panic when things don't work out as planned.

For example, maybe you did not get the score that you wanted on your SAT the first time that you took it. Do not be defined by what you didn't accomplish. Instead, go to www.collegeboard.org and take the online SAT practice test multiple times; go to the library and checkout a SAT prep book; take a SAT prep class if it is offered at your high school; watch instruction videos on YouTube; and apply to take the test again until you accomplish your goal. When you find yourself struggling ask yourself this question: "How well am I utilizing my resources?"

I remember as sophomore in high school, I took a chemistry course. One of my favorite things about this class was that my instructor would give us group labs that consisted of formulating a hypothesis, making an observation, identifying controls/ constants and finding the dependent and independent variables in an experiment. I loved this class, and I always performed well during this portion. Another one of my favorite things about this class was my chemistry teacher. She had one of the most welcoming smiles and brightest spirits. I remember her because of her great lecturing ability and the fact that she made her chemistry class very interesting and fun. There was never a dull moment.

At one point during the semester, my grades dropped significantly due to my test scores. I was never a great test-taker. I've always been more of a hands-on, practical person. Tests never reflected the knowledge I had gained. I want to stop here and remind you that it's always important to identify an area of weakness that you might have and try to communicate it as fast as possible to a person that can help you. If you don't tell a trusted individual about a struggle you are facing, you will find yourself constantly avoiding problems in life and isolating yourself from other people. Building up enough courage to confront a situation will not only help you excel in the area that you need help in, but you will feel much more confident about yourself knowing that you are taking an action to overcome limitations that you might have.

I pulled my teacher to the side one day after class and told her that I was really concerned about my grade in her class. I was aware that I wasn't performing well on my test, and I wanted to know if there was anything that I could do to improve my grade. Also, I remember communicating this to her way before it was time for her to submit the final grades that went on my report at the end of the semester. This is another important habit to follow. Effective communication is something that is crucial to your success. You won't know how to succeed unless you ask. If you wait too long to ask, you might miss out on an opportunity. There is nothing wrong with being specific and direct. The most successful people ask questions because they know that asking questions yields solutions to problems.

After communicating this concern to my chemistry teacher, she was beyond enthusiastic and offered me a solution to help improve my grade. She informed me that due to her schedule, she often arrived at school at 6:00 a.m. every morning. She recommended that I could come in roughly an hour and a half before class (on the days that I had her class) and she would be willing to review my test with me, in hopes that we would both see an improvement in my performance. The only issue was that her class didn't begin until 7:25 a.m., which meant that in order for me to arrive for tutoring at 6:00 a.m., I would have to be willing to sacrifice and wake up at 5:00 a.m. just to be at the school on time. This was an issue for me because I did not catch the bus to school. I would have to rely on my mother to wake up two hours earlier than she usually did just to take me to school for tutoring.

After talking to my mom about the situation, she agreed to wake up earlier to take me to school. She did this every other day. This continued for about three weeks straight. While in tutoring, I began to retain more information. I would take my work home and review my notes over and over again. I even had a chance to study with other students that were in tutoring as well. The more I went to tutoring, the more my grades started to reflect. I saw higher test scores, and eventually I passed the class.

This goes to show you that perfect practice makes perfect. Striving toward a goal followed by implementing a plan of action is crucial to your success in high school. You can do anything that you put your mind to. Consistency towards your goals is key. Just remember, if you ever experience a setback while in high school, whether it is a drop in your grades; conflict with your peers; family issues; or not enough support from your environment, becoming complacent and stagnant is not the answer. You must persevere because you are destined for greatness! If I would not have shown up for tutoring because it was too early in the morning, it would have resulted in me not passing my tests. I had to become uncomfortable in order to achieve my goal.

Right now, wherever you are, I want you to ask yourself: "What is something or someone in my life that is holding me back from applying myself?" Here is something that I want you to remember. You can't control what other people say or do, but you can control your own actions. One way to ensure that you are always taking the best action against any situation in life is to stop trying to be perfect. Instead, focus on the process. When you become obsessed with every little mistake you make or others that are around you, it can become your own roadblock to success.

Take time to reflect on some of your achievements in high school or in your personal life. I recommend keeping a journal of them. If you won an award, write it down. If you passed a test, write it down. If your basketball team won a game, frame the certificate. Following these steps will help you become better at persevering.

Chapter 2
Be the Change You Want to see

"Don't chase success. Decide to make a difference and success will find you." ~ Jon Gordon

It doesn't matter who you are or where you are from, you can do anything that you put your mind to. Sometimes you might find it difficult to actually believe in yourself because of negative external influences. These negative influences are what I like to call limiting beliefs. Limiting beliefs are negative thought patterns that you've accepted as truth, but in reality, these thoughts are false. When you embrace these beliefs, it can cause you to live below you potential. They can also cause you to have a hard time fully applying yourself because you feel that you can't accomplish your goal.

For example, these are a few limiting beliefs:

- In order to be considered "smart," you need a 4.0 GPA.

- You are too young to accomplish your dream of becoming an actor, singer, model, doctor, lawyer or entrepreneur.

- You can't be a successful athlete because you're too short.

- You can't be a successful model because you're too fat or skinny.

- Because your parents do not have a lot of money, you can't go to college or you won't ever amount to anything.

- Your future/success is determined by your parents, teachers, and guidance counselors.

Maybe these are some of the limiting beliefs that you have experienced. Maybe you can or cannot relate to them. Everybody's situation is different. But after reading this book, you will feel more comfortable addressing these limiting beliefs because I'm going to show you how to build confidence in yourself based off one of my life experiences.

Track Team Tryout

In my sophomore year of high school, I thought that it would be a cool idea to try out for the track team. My only background in sports was when I played basketball in the 5th grade for the local YMCA. Other than that, I did not have too much history. I thought it would be a great idea because I noticed that it high school, the guys that played sports such as football, baseball, basketball and track were much more muscular than I was. They looked strong, and so on the inside, I started to compare myself with them. I figured that if I ran track, I would become taller (that was one limiting belief right there). I also thought that I would fit in with the other kids that were athletes and have more attention from girls.

It is important to know that your validation or worth should not come from other people. Personally, I believe that validation comes from God. Only the creator can validate who you are because you are a part of His creation. Never compare your life with other people. There is nothing wrong with admiring people's hard work, talent, and success. You can even emulate it but do it in your own way. Don't try to be like them. Armed with the knowledge you have learned from others, try to be like yourself.

So, I tried out for the team. After school, I went directly to the field to stretch, practice, warm up and go over routines. Mind you, I hadn't made the team yet. It was preseason, and I showed up to the practices so that I could condition and do drills. One day, my coach wanted the team to do a 100M sprint from one side of the track to the other. My teammates and I all lined up in our lanes. The coach got his whistle in his hand and yelled, "On your mark, get set, go!" He blew the whistle, and I could feel the strong wind blowing just like when I was riding my bike down the street trying to impress my older neighbors. It felt as if I had gained an endorphin rush in my body.

I started to get into the rhythm of running as my feet flew on and off the ground effortlessly until about 30 seconds later. I noticed in my peripheral vision that the other guys on my team were moving much faster and progressing just a little bit closer to the finish than I was. Have you been in a small, compact car? You know that feeling when a large semi-trailer truck pulls up next to you at a red light? When the light turns green, both vehicles begin to accelerate but inside the small compact car, you feel like you are going in reverse. That's exactly how it felt while I was running on the track.

By this time, I realized that the entire team had already ran to the other side of the track, while I had barely even made it half way. The sad part about it was that the team had to run to the finish line and then turn around and run back to where we had initially started. I was a complete a mess. When I got back home that night, I reflected on what had happened earlier that day. My biggest takeaway was that I hate playing sports. I don't enjoy the hard labor. I would much rather use my brain to work on something that I'm good at versus sweating. I realized that athletic ability was not in my DNA. The lesson is that what might work for somebody else, might not always work for you. Your strengths may not be someone else's strengths, and vice versa.

The Formula for Achieving Results

The truth is, we all are passionate about something, whether it is a sports teams, music, dancing, acting, or a subject that means a lot to us (political agenda, family, personal interest). Somehow these things stem from a motive that drives us to perform an action. The question is whether our passion for something increases or limits our productivity. You might listen to music every day and the songs that you listen to make you want to stand up and dance or bop your head back and forth. Songs are great, and music is great. That might be something that you are passionate about. But after listening to music, you may realize that two hours have passed. The music sparked your emotion. You were in the moment and felt ignited, but your productivity was wasted because when the music stops, there is no action plan for following your passion.

Sometimes, what you consider to be the best plan for following your passion, may not always be what's best for you. Just think about it. Is the two hours you spent listening to music adding any value to you or is it holding you back? Could you have used those two hours to produce a track or write a song? These are the actions that produce results.

As a high school student, it can be difficult to know exactly what you want to do after graduation. Some students just know that they want to go to college to be a doctor. Why? Because they've had that same dream and aspiration ever since the age of 5. Every day since then, they've read books, studied and asked questions pertaining to what it takes to be a successful doctor. Either their parents were doctors, or they surrounded themselves with other doctors. They know how long it takes to go to medical school, how long their residency is and the time it takes until they receive their license. After all these years of determination, they start to put forth the effort and day by day, they see the results.

It is important to follow results because results are proven. When you see an outcome of your work, you can personally say that your results have been tested and tried. That's one important thing to remember as a high school student. Producing results show that you have expertise and experience, which are two things that no one can ever take from you. My question for you is, "What actionable steps are you taking today to get you closer to where you want to be tomorrow?"

Determination + Effort = Results

When you take the necessary steps towards anything that you set your mind to, you will accomplish your goals. If you hate playing sports, then do not force yourself to play sports. When you make yourself do something that you do not want to do, then you are wasting time. You are affecting your integrity because you're not staying true to yourself. You only have one life, so make it count. Do you want to know how you can become the best at anything? Focus on what YOU want. Work hard every day towards achieving YOUR goals, and then you will begin to see results. Once you see results, you'll begin to realize the things that you are passionate about. In this next chapter, I will be discussing how I focused on my goals in high school and worked hard until I saw results.

Chapter 3
Stay Ahead of the Game

"The secret of getting ahead is getting started." ~ *Mark Twain*

I was not raised with a silver spoon in my mouth. I have an awesome mother who did not have a lot of money, which is why I am grateful the many things that I have now. In high school, I faced numerous decisions. One of them was deciding my next step after high school. These are some of the questions I would ask myself:

- What will I do beyond high school?

- Will I ever get a job?

- Will I have enough money to sustain myself?

On top of those decisions, my mother had just recently lost her job as a banker for over 11 years. This happened during my sophomore year in high school and because of that, we struggled financially, which caused a great deal of mental strain. My mother's financial struggles showed me that it was going to be up to me to create a better future for my life. One night, I remember praying and asking God to show me how I could create a better life for myself because I did not want to have to worry about not having money after high school.

Start with the End in Mind

A few months later, I noticed a building under construction about two blocks away from my high school. I walked past it everyday on my way to school. Finally, one day I walked up to the construction site and saw a wooden stand with a sheet of paper attached to it. It was Chick-Fil-A job posting. They were looking to hire a part time team member. At the time, I was only 15 years old and to work, my mother wanted me to be 16. Despite my age, I knew that eventually I would apply for the position.

About a year later, I walked into the Chick-Fil-A restaurant and submitted my application. On the spot, one of the managers asked if I could come in for an interview the following week, and I said, "Yes." After I came in for the interview, I was told that it would be a group interview. I would sit with other applicants, and we would talk to each other for about 10 minutes. Then, after we finished talking, we would say something to describe the person sitting next to us. One of the things that I had mentioned was that I attended Maury High School, which was about two blocks down from Chick-Fil-A. About a week later, I got the call that I was hired, and I started working at Chick-Fil-A during the second semester of my junior year in high school.

When I asked the marketing director why I was hired, she mentioned it was because of my great personality. She said that it made sense to hire me, since I attended the high school down the street from the restaurant. The information I shared at the interview ended up working out in my favor. Sometimes, you will find opportunities come to you simply because you were in the right place at the right time. When these opportunities come, don't ignore them. Since this was my first job, I knew that I wanted to make the most of every moment. To do this, I created a schedule that I included below so that I could maintain a work/life balance.

Create a Daily Schedule

- Wake up at 5:30-5:45 a.m.

- Spiritual devotion 5:45 - 6:05 a.m.

- Get dressed/eat breakfast 6:10 a.m. - 6:45 a.m.

- Head to school 6:50 a.m.

- Classes begin 7:25 a.m. - 2:00 p.m.

- Start on homework 2:15 - 2:55p.m.

- Work schedule- 3:00 p.m. - 8:00 p.m.

- Finish homework 8:30- 9:30 p.m.

- Bed by 10:00 p.m.

Typically, I would plan my schedule the night before. As a junior in high school, I volunteered for several non-profit organizations. As you can imagine, sometimes my schedule would change, and I would have to adapt to a new schedule. However, I believe that creating a daily schedule will help you stay more focused. You will produce more good habits and have an efficient routine that will give you more control over your day. Always plan what time you will wake up and eat breakfast because it helps you have clarity throughout the day. Also, drink plenty of water. My schedule will be different from yours, but it is important to note on your schedule how you plan to allocate your time. At times, school work can be very demanding and rigorous. Try to be as organized as possible by planning your schedule the night before so that you will be able to meet any deadlines that you might have for school or work.

Capitalize on Opportunities

During this time, things started to get a little better for me because I was committed to my full-time obligations as a student in high school and a part time employee at Chick-Fil-A, where I worked roughly 20 hours a week as a cashier. My mom was still struggling to find employment and because she was not working, we had to relocate and move in with a family member. She was optimistic throughout the entire process, which motivated me to work harder.

One day, while I was doing some research online, I came across an application for an internship program called NEL (Norfolk Emerging Leaders). I heard of this program before, but I never considered applying because you had to be 16 years or older. As a NEL Intern, I committed to an eight-week paid internship while working for the city of Norfolk. I chose to work for a department that matched my future career interest, which included:

Budget and Grants Assistants	Public Works Specialists
Finance Assistants	Recreation Assistants
Library Assistants	Student Artists
Office Assistants	Utility Technicians

This opportunity captured my attention because I saw it as a way to work alongside city employees and gain knowledge and valuable work experience. I knew that to be successful, I needed to network with other like-minded individuals. I was willing to learn from others, so I decided to take a chance and complete an online application. Although my mom and I were still struggling financially, I did not let that setback prevent me from applying. After I submitted my application, I knew that I would be selected for the internship. There was no doubt in mind that I would not be selected.

Sell Yourself

After waiting patiently for about two months, I received an email, notifying me that I was selected to proceed to the second round, which was the interview process. This process consisted of a group interview. About 6-8 other applicants and myself would sit in front of a group of interviewers. We were asked a series of questions, and then the selection committee would decide which 2-5 would be selected for the summer internship. I knew that this was my chance to sell myself. Selling yourself means that you highlight your qualities that make you stand out from the crowd. During the interview, I walked with a smile. I greeted every interviewer with a firm handshake and as I took my seat, I sat up straight and made eye contact with them. The other applicants and myself were only asked about 5 questions, but the rest of the time we just listened to the program coordinator tell us about the program. Here are a few tips that I recommend when it comes to selling yourself.

1. <u>Know your brand-</u> Your brand is your reputation or your story. Every individual has one. Think of it like this. What is the first thing you think of when you hear the name, Michael Jordan? Basketball. What is the first thing you think of when you hear the name Bill Gates? Microsoft. In high school, many of you might be involved in extra circular activities. If you play sports, then people might refer to you as an athlete. If you perform in plays, then people might refer to you as an actor/actress. If you make straight A's, then people might refer to you as a smart student. Your brand is what people say about you when you are not in the room.

One of the best ways in high school to develop your brand is to create a resume. But wait! In order to create a resume, you have to put something on it or else it would just be a blank sheet of paper. Your resume can highlight your recent work and volunteer experience as well as enhance your brand. Before you put anything on your resume, ask yourself, "Can I explain everything that is on here?" You should know your resume better than anybody else in the room, and when you are asked a question regarding something on it, you should be able to give a solid answer. Here is an example of the resume that I used to apply to the Norfolk Emerging Leader Program.

Isaiah Swift

[Address, City, ST ZIP Code] | [Telephone] | [Email]

Objective

- Innovative professional with experience in customer service and sales. Highly motivated self-starter, who is eager to work in a career where my skill set and knowledge can be utilized effectively.

Education

Advanced Diploma | June 2016 | Maury High School

- National Honor Society

- DECA (President)

- Future Business Leaders of America

- National Society of High School Scholars

Skills & Abilities

SALES – DRIVEN AND EFFECTIVE

COMMUNICATION – TECHNICAL WRITING, ADVANCED COMPOSITION

SOFTWARE – MICROSOFT OFFICE, WEB SOFTWARE, VIDEO PRODUCTION

Experience

CASHIER/HOST | CHIK-FIL-A | MARCH 2015-PRESENT

- Responsible for taking and giving out orders from the customers

- Required to balance cash drawers, answer questions from the customers with regards to the menu items and other special services offered by the restaurant

- Accompany guests to their seats in a very sociable manner while upholding the flow of customers arriving and leaving the restaurant

References

AVAILABLE UPON REQUEST

As you can tell, my resume gives clearer detail as to who I am, what school I attend, what my job objective is, etc. Don't worry about having two pages worth of experience. Employers know that you are still in high school. Instead, utilize the resources that you already have.

What are some ways that you can enhance your resume?

Start by listing your **5 hobbies** (where do you spend most of your time?), **5 skills** (what are you good at?) and **5 volunteer experience**s (do you dedicate time to serve a local charity, church or hospital?), and then narrow it down by choosing the top 2-3 in each category to include as a part of your resume. Once your resume is finished, show it to a trusted individual such as a parent, personal finance teacher or your guidance counselor to review.

Outwork Your Competition

After the interview was over, I knew that I would receive a call letting me know that I was selected for the internship. Employers like to see ambitious young people. It's never too late to improve your work ethic. At 17-years-old, I was already on track to receive an advanced diploma, while working a part-time job and volunteering in the community. One day, I was sitting in class and my teacher mentioned one of her co-workers was hiring for a part-time clean up job during the summer. He was looking for talented, bright students that were willing to roll up their sleeves and sweep up trash at festivals every other weekend during the summer. I spent the entire class wondering if I could manage working a third job during the summer. Just the thought of it made me dizzy, but

I liked the idea of working three jobs during the summer because nobody else was doing it at the time.

I worked 5 days a week at NEL from 7:00 a.m.- 3:00 p.m. I worked 3-5 days a week at Chick-Fil-A from 5:30 p.m. – 11:00 p.m. And then, I worked about two weekends a month during the summer, typically anywhere from 5-10 hour shifts. After class, I immediately went to the guidance office to speak to my teacher's co-worker. I explained to him what I had just heard in class, and I told him that I was interested in working a summer job. I had the confidence and skills because of my current work experience, and I knew that I could handle any task. He took down my contact information and told me that he would reach out to me shortly.

Why Outworking your Competition is Important

- Think about it this way. When you get a job in high school, you are in the top 20% of students that are working. When you get a second job during the summer, that puts you within the top 1% of students in your class that are working.

- In a world of capitalism, it is all about competition. Your job as a high school student is to study the blueprint of a successful person. From the time I stepped foot into my first job at Chick-Fil-A, I started to study the owner. I watched his every move, from the clothes he had on, how he interacted with other employees, what time he would come to the restaurant, to who would he ask to do a task, and what he would eat. Why? Because he was my target of what a successful person looked like. I wanted to understand what he might've done if he was a 17-year-old with a job.

A Method to My Madness

You might be thinking, "Why did he work three jobs during the summer?" Trust me, at times, I was wondering the same thing. But the truth is, I wasn't lazy. I had to be moving. I hated staying in the house all day, and I was not going to waste another summer watching TV and playing video games. I know that some students in high school have more responsibility than others and working one job or more than one job is not feasible. Others may lack the motivation or don't have a strong work ethic. Others may be like me and are being raised in a single parent home and don't have access lot of money. Some students might be responsible for watching their younger siblings after school, taking care of one of their family members or committed to playing sports. If you are 16 or older, I highly recommend you start working at your first job during the summer or during the school year. Please consult your parent/guardian or guidance counselor to determine the best fit schedule.

These are some of the valuable tools that my first job gave me:

Earning Money Offers an Opportunity for Financial Education

- When I received my first paycheck, I noticed that federal taxes, social security and Medicare taxes were all withheld from my paycheck.

- I had to learn how to create a budget so that I could properly allocate my paycheck. Each pay period I recommend that you prepare a budget to ensure that your money is not wasted.

- Give 10% to your local church or a charity of your choice. You can never go wrong by supporting a good cause.

- Save 20% of your paycheck and place it into a savings account.

How to Build Valuable Work Experience

- In the workforce and even in the business world, it's not so much about what you know but who you know. A college degree is very valuable, but it's even more valuable with a background full of work experience because it shows you can balance work and education at the same time.

- At this stage in life, you need to interact with as many people as you can. Working a job will teach you how to provide quality customer service that can be beneficial when you begin your career or start a business.

Learn from your mistakes

- Everyone messes up, but your response will determine if you grow from that mistake. There were plenty of times I messed up a customer's order or could have confronted an issue with a team member in a different way. Having a job will teach you what to do after you make mistakes. Always remember to Try. Learn. Repeat. (TLR)

- Mistakes + Lessons Learned = Education

Focus on my Priorities

- Working in high school helps you maintain a sense of responsibility because it shows that you can be independent, which is necessary to be successful in college.

- Having a job in high school can increase your chances of staying out of trouble because working enhances your productivity.

- Start with the end in mind. The earlier you start to develop work ethic, the better. Your first job will simply lay the ground work for your future.

Chapter 4
Go the Extra Mile

"Opportunities are never lost; someone will take the one you miss." ~ Author Unknown

One of my most memorable classes was personal finance because of my teacher, Mrs. V. At the beginning of the school year, Mrs. V took time to study every student in her class and evaluate them. At the end of the day, she would reach out to their parent guardian and say something to edify the student. Now, in the household that I grew up in, my mother reared me in the right direction, so in high school I kept to myself and did not get into a lot of trouble. My mother was very aware of what I was doing in and outside of school because of our close relationship, and she raised me to be respectful and walk in integrity. So, when Mrs. V called my mother that day to tell her how I was doing in class, I knew that my mom would listen closely to what Mrs. V was going to say.

I overheard Mrs. V telling my mom that she wished she had twenty Isaiah Swifts in her classroom. Mrs. V said that I was polite, and I would always contribute to class topics. In my opinion, she started the year off right and was hands-down, one of my favorite teachers. Throughout the year, Mrs. V was always willing to write recommendation letters for me and tell me about upcoming opportunities that she thought I might be interested in.

The Stock Market Challenge

One day in class, Mrs. V walked up to me and said, "Isaiah I have an opportunity that I think will be great for you. It's called the Bank of America Stock Market Challenge. She asked if I would be interested in attending, and I told her I would definitely be there. The Bank of America Stock Market Challenge was an event where local high school students competed in a Wall Street stock simulation to build the biggest stock portfolio. This event was sponsored by Bank of America and took place inside a conference room at the Marriot Hotel.

When I attended this event, I participated in two trading sessions with a team of about eight people. Our objective was to make trades and buy stocks. Each team started with $100,000 to invest and competed with teams from other schools to see which team could gain the biggest return on their investment. Inside the conference room, there were about a dozen standing tables, and each group would gather around the table. At the center of the table, there was a remote control that allowed us to click "buy" when we wanted to invest in a stock or click "sell" if we predicted that the price of a stock would go down. At the front of room, there as a big screen that allowed every participant to see which stocks we would be trading. The event lasted for about two hours.

Imagine a room filled with about 150 high school students that are given $100,000 worth of play money to compete in a game to see which group could win the most money. That was one of the most energetic moments I ever experienced in my life. People's emotions were erupting. It was fun. Although my team was not one of the overall winners, I would compete all over again if I knew the experience would be that good.

As I prepared to leave the event for the day, I remember noticing a flyer laying on the ground. This is what the flyer read:

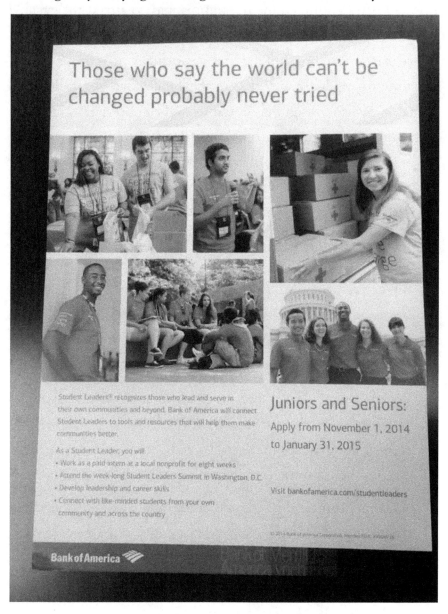

The first word that came to my mind was "Wow!" This internship for Bank of America looked amazing. I couldn't believe that an opportunity like this one even existed. Earlier in the book, I mentioned the importance of capitalizing on opportunities. What if, when Mrs. V. offered me the opportunity to attend the event, I would have said, "No," "I can't make it" or "I'm too busy." I would have missed out on the first opportunity, which was having the time of my life competing in the Stock Market Challenge. I would have also missed out on the second opportunity, which was discovering a flyer on the ground for a Bank of America internship. I was so eager to apply to this program, although, I didn't know much about it. I just knew that in life, if you want to be successful, it's not about what you know but who you know.

Key Points:

1. **Be active outside the classroom**: Participating in events forces you to engage with others, and you can include these experiences on your resume when it comes to applying for jobs, scholarships and colleges.

2. **Learn a new skill**: I had no prior knowledge in regards to building a stock portfolio; however, just by attending this event, I was exposed to the basics and got to see first-hand how it would be if I were to trade professionally.

3. **Value the opinion of trusted individuals**: Whether it's your mentor, spiritual leader, coach or parent, pay attention to these people who are around you because they have spent hours observing your habits. They know who you are, and they

believe in you. Good teachers will pull out the best in their students, and if a teacher takes time to recommend you for a scholarship, conference and/or event, they must see something good in you.

4. **Pay attention to your environment**: Everywhere that I go, one of the first things that I do is try to get an understanding of my surroundings. I take note of the name of the street I'm on, the time of the day, the people I meet to include their names and physical features, etc. At this event, I noticed a flyer laying on the ground. It caught my attention, so I picked it up. Noticing this one piece of paper was able to change the course of my life. Read on as I explain how.

Later that night, I went online and tried to research as much as I could regarding the Bank of America Student Leader program. I found that this this was an eight-week paid summer internship, where I would work for a local non-profit organization in my community to improve my workforce and leadership skills. Also, I would assist non-profit executives with various aspects of the business while learning about how a non-profit organization functions. The most interesting fact was, during the eight-week program, I would attend a leadership summit for one week. I would meet government officials, motivational speakers and roughly 200 Bank of America student leaders from around the country. A few of the requirements for the internship were that you had to be a junior or senior in high school, you had to provide two recommendation letters and you had to be a legal resident of the U.S. Also, the applicant had to answer a series of questions describing in detail your strengths and weakness, volunteer experience and future career goals and aspirations.

Use Your Mistakes as Motivation, Not Excuses

What do you do when something happens in your life that doesn't go as planned? Previously, my natural response has been to freak out or isolate myself. In reality, we cannot always control our situation, but we can control our response. I read a book entitled, *Basic Instructions Before Leaving the Earth* which stated, "Faith without works is dead." This means if what you say you believe does not result in action, then you probably don't even believe in what you are saying. The silent implication is that you won't get anywhere in life, if you give up after the first try. Your results are preceded by your actions.

Unfortunately, I was not selected for the Bank of America Student Leaders program that year. The decisions were released about three months after I applied. Although, I met the criteria for a few categories, I realized afterwards, that when I submitted my application, there were some things that I could have done better. Listed below are two of the most important missing elements. I want to emphasize that you do not need these characteristics to be accepted into the program. These are just some of the observations that I've seen from current and past student leaders. In addition, knowing this information will enhance your application, but it does not guarantee your acceptance into the program.

1. Community Service Work

2. Effective Writing Skills

Why is Community Service Important?

1. Volunteering allows students to develop social and technical skills that cannot be obtained in the classroom. You get a feel for different environments and you can learn about other people's situations.

2. I would assume that most people reading this book have a home, clothes on their back and food to eat. The same is not true for most people living in third world countries. In comparison to their living conditions, we are not lucky, we are blessed.

3. Did you know that just by volunteering for a non-profit organization in high school, you can expose yourself to a wide variety of networks? Volunteering reflects who you are as a person, which is something that employers and college admission officers would love to see. You will develop people skills.

Why are Effective Writing Skills Important?

1. Your Career: Knowing basic writing skills are important and will be beneficial to you as it relates to employment. When writing an email to your boss, you have to differentiate between your friend. Most of the time, teens are so used to tweeting and texting that they don't always spell out words or proof read. Knowing this can either hurt or help your future career. Having writing skills can help you come across as someone who is knowledgeable about what they are writing.

2. Credibility: Students that have good writing skills are seen as more credible. Imagine sending an email to your teacher, submitting a scholarship, or filling out a job application and its filled with grammatical errors and several typos. No one will take you seriously. Always remember to spell check and read over the content before you send it.

3. Improved Speaking Skills: The more you practice writing, the better writing skills you will develop. Writing can also help improve the way you verbally communicate. You will start to develop an expanded vocabulary, and people will have a better impression of you.

Chapter 5
Make it Count

There were some times in high school that I felt like giving up. I felt like quitting. We did not have a lot of money. My mother was unemployed, and we had to move from our apartment. My mother's car was repossessed, and we had to live with family until my mom could find another apartment. On top of that, I had demands in high school; deadlines that I had to meet for grades, scholarships, SAT and ACT; volunteer commitments and I worked a part time job. Many people ask me how I pushed through. What did I tell myself to get through the day? Was I attentive in class? This is my response. High school is what you make it.

If you perceive school as being a place where you HAVE to learn, then you're in trouble. School is a place where you GET to learn, not just in the classroom, but outside the classroom. It is possible to expand your knowledge as well. Whatever experiences you have, make them count. Don't waste your time complaining or wishing it was different. Whether it is a good or bad experience, be determined to make every triumph, challenge, and lesson count. Below are some of my favorites experiences of what I did to make it count while I was a student in high school.

My Time Management Advice

"The key is in not spending time, but in investing it." ~Stephen R. Covey

- Keep a to-do list: Plan your day the night before. Try to write down as much as you need to remember (start and end time of classes, practice time for after school sports or activities, work schedule, homework, or time needed to study). Set a time that you will complete each task. Literally write how much time you will spend next to each class. If you make your schedule a day in advance, you will discover each day you are more productive.

- One way to get more done throughout the day is to simply arrive early. I remember arriving to school at least 20 minutes before my classes started just so that I could have enough time to follow up with my counselor on the status of my grades, go to the library to print, read a chapter of a book, or stop by a teacher's office to ask a question.

Side note: Teachers love to see ambitious students. When you are working on your homework and you come to a question that you do not understand, instead of not making any effort, make a note of the question, plan to arrive early to class the next day or schedule an appointment (email your teacher in advance), and ask if you can review that question with your teacher .Chances are if the assignment is due, your teacher would be more willing to help you versus penalize you and cut you some slack when they grade your test. Making good use of your time can go a long way.

Stay Organized

- Whenever a teacher would give an assignment in class, I would write my name and date on each assignment. I kept a folder for each class and I would arrange each assignment in order according to its due date. So, if I needed to find my test review change from last class, I could find it more easily, simply because I kept my assignments in order by the date.

- Some of my teachers used to lecture or go off on tangents. Most of the time, they would try to incorporate real world examples into their lesson plans, so I would also keep sticky notes just in case they said something that I thought would benefit me in the future.

Join an Organization

You don't have to have a 4.0 GPA in order to join an organization in high school. However, it is still a good idea to maintain at least a 3.3 or higher. As a high school student, I took advantage of just about every opportunity I could find. During my sophomore year, I was selected to be a part of the National Honor Society because my GPA was a 3.3. One of my most memorable experiences in high school was my time spent in the National Honor Society. Every student had to commit to at least two or more volunteer commitments every semester. I remember participating in an angel tree event, where I was assigned to purchase a gift for a little girl that was in the Children Kings Daughter's (CHKD) hospital. I don't say this to brag, but what I did for her was something that I would want somebody to do for me. I went to Macy's to buy her an outfit. Just the feeling of taking time during the Christmas season to take the focus off of myself and donate a new outfit to a child in a hospital was life changing for me. Now, I'm constantly challenging myself to do more for others, not just during the Christmas holiday but year-round. Being a part of this organization allowed me to have a life changing experience. Remember, high school is what you make it, so make it count.

Make High School Your Priority

There were times when my commitments seemed overwhelming. In those times, my mom would remind me that school was my only priority and it goes by fast. Some adults wish that they could go back in time and do high school all over again. I will tell you the same thing that my mom told me. Your only main responsibility as a student is to apply yourself and take advantage of resources that are offered to you. You don't have to be one of those students that carries five textbooks in their backpack, sits in the front of class and raises their hand for every question. But you do have to make your success as a student your main focus from the time you are a freshman until you graduate. You need a high school diploma to go to college or start your career. Even if you choose not to go to college, being involved in high school can help you socially develop because you can meet new people and discover your identity.

Get Involved

As a senior, I served as a branch manager of a student run credit union called Commodore Branch. Commodore Branch was a subsidiary of Port Alliance Federal Credit Union. Port Alliance was a fully functioning credit union where students were hired as "employees" to work inside a kiosk set up in the school cafeteria during the lunch shifts. During the lunch shifts, I would perform duties such as accepting member applications from students and processing withdrawals and deposits. Through this experience, I became more financially educated and a better marketer. In an effort to increase attraction and promote our branch, the co-branch manager and myself would reach out to local companies like Chick-Fil-A, Starbucks and Tropical Smoothie. We would ask if they could provide us with gift cards to use as incentives for students that open an account. Once we received an approval, we would create and design flyers and post them around the school.

The branch liaison and personal finance teacher, Mrs. Nobles, was very resourceful. She would sometimes drive and pick up the promotional items for us. She assisted in the designs for the branch and was one of the teachers that I asked to review my resume. She was also a great mentor to the co- branch manager and myself. Without her, I would have never had a great reputation in high school. She always spoke highly of me. You never know who's watching you so get involved. Many times, teachers talk amongst themselves, and a good compliment about your character can go a long way.

Find A Volunteer Organization that Interests You

"We make a living by what we get, but we make a life by what we give." ~ Winston Churchill

One day, I met a teacher who was a liaison for an after-school volunteer program where students would dedicate time on a Saturday to volunteer for a nonprofit organization called the Roc Solid Foundation. The Roc Solid Foundation is a non-profit organization that builds custom playsets for kids ages 1-8 that are recovering from pediatric cancer. Through their "Play it Forward Initiative," kids between ages 8-18 receive a complete room makeover. After the teacher explained this to me, I immediately put my name on the signup sheet.

The teacher provided me with the address to attend one of the room makeovers for a guy in high school. The following Saturday, I went to his house and saw a table labeled, "Roc Solid Foundation," and walked inside. There were about 20 volunteers in attendance. My job as a volunteer was to pass a brick and help out in any way that I could. As a volunteer, each individual played a part. We literally had to completely demolish his current room and renovate it. The only thing that we didn't throw away were his clothes and personal belongings.

The volunteers had an onsite project coordinator and interior designer that completely renovated this teen's bedroom. Roc Solid even covered the family's expenses to go away for a day. He did not have any idea what was happening. At the end of the day, he and his family came back to the house in a limo that Roc Solid provided. As we all waited outside with cameras in our hands ready to capture the moment, he and his family got out of the limousine to people smiling, cheering, crying and rejoicing for him.

He walked into his bedroom to see a completely redesigned room with a flat screen TV, a desk to do his homework, and a guitar hung up on the wall because he loved to play the guitar. The entire room was designed in the color blue, which was his favorite color. I was so moved by this event. I remembered him telling me which high school he went to, and it wasn't too far from mine. Several months later, I contacted his guidance counselor because I was trying to get in contact with his mother to see how his progress was coming with treatment.

This was her response from the event:

Hello, Mr. Swift,

I understand you are trying to get in touch with us. I cannot tell you how appreciative we were for everything that Roc Solid did for my son. It was truly an amazing and humbling experience for us as well. He could not believe people he did not even know would do what they did. He was overwhelmed by the kindness and compassion of people like yourself.

As of now, he is in remission and we hope for him to remain that way from here on out! He has a full head of hair again (except it is slightly curly!). He is back to his sports activities, swimming and has even decided to give Lacrosse a try.

We realize how fortunate we are for his good prognosis. Again, thank you and may you and yours be truly blessed!

Just from a conversation with a teacher, I discovered a volunteer opportunity that had such a profound impact on my life. Knowing that I did my small part made all the difference in the world.

Chapter 6
Never Give Up

"It always seems impossible until it's done." ~ *Nelson Mandela*

Setbacks You Might be facing as a student

1. Financial issues- inability to pay for senior dues, ACT/SAT, school lunch, college admission fees

2. Punctuality- getting to class on time

3. Public Speaking

4. Feeling inadequate compared to your classmates

5. Poor grades

Ways to overcome Setbacks

If your family is going through financial problems and you do not have the money to pay for the cost of school related test expenses, I highly recommend setting up a meeting with your guidance counselor to see if you qualify for fee waivers. The majority of the time you can qualify for a fee waiver if:

1. You are enrolled in a free or reduced lunch program at your school.

2. If your family receives public assistance.

3. If you live in public housing or foster care.

4. If your household income level falls below the USDA levels for reduced price lunches. Contact your guidance counselor ASAP to see if you qualify for a waiver.

One thing my mentor told me was that if you are on time, then you are employable. If you are employable, then you will always have a job. Get rid of the myth, "Better late than never." In the real world, that doesn't apply. Everybody might find themselves in a unique position. Maybe you can't get to school on time because your parents bring you to school, you have to walk in the rain, illness in the family, etc. These are all valid reasons, but something as simple as explaining these valid reasons to your guidance counselor or teachers can keep you from being penalized. You can have your parent write a note to the school addressing the reason why you were late to class or you can obtain proof from a doctor as to why you couldn't make class. The school will then provide you with an excused absence. This simple action can help reduce the amount of days that you miss school so that you won't fail any of your courses.

Public speaking is a skill that many students are going to be required to practice while in high school. Whether you are giving a presentation, doing a job interview or introducing a speaker at a ceremony, this skill is essential. One of the things that I found is that many students get nervous when they have to speak in front of large crowds.

My advice is to:

1. Practice speaking in front of a mirror, as you rehearse what you say. Pay attention to your hand gestures, eye contact and pitch of your voice. Continue to speak over and over again until you can find your rhythm. Whatever makes you comfortable. This practice will help you to be calm when you have to speak before an audience.

2. Ask for a family member or friend to read and review your speech. Speaking directly in front of another person will help alleviate stress the more you practice.

Maybe you feel ashamed or embarrassed regarding your physical size and you start to compare yourself with others, or you compare yourself to others who score higher grades, wear better clothes.

My advice is to:

1. Write down your fears. Address what they are and then take that sheet of paper, rip it out and throw it away. That action signifies that you don't accept that fear or negative belief into your mind.

Sometimes the smartest students can find themselves underperforming in their grades, especially as a freshman or sophomore in high school. Those first two years are the most crucial to your academic performance as college admission recruiters look at these year.

Actions to improve your grades:

1. Whether in math, English or history, figure out which subject or subjects are most difficult. Identify your area of weakness.

2. Talk to your teachers. Recall in the first chapter when I said that you should be afraid to ask for help (tutoring, ask for instructor to repeat questions, extra credit etc.).

3. Start to pay more attention in class. Use a highlighter to highlight test review questions. Sometimes it requires action on your part. Ask to change seats in class and move closer to the front. Don't allow your mind to daydream in class. Simply focus.

4. Don't wait until the last minute. If you don't address the issue with your grades ahead of time, you may miss out on the opportunity to improve your grade or it might be more difficult for your teacher to work with you, considering the student to teacher ratio is on average 1:17 in each class.

5. Figure out what works for you. Have you found your effective studying style? For example, you might find it easier to work with classmates. If this is the case, form a study group so that you have someone else there to motivate you.

3 Ways I Stay Motived:

1. One of the first things that I do is pray. I believe that prayer helps me personally to stay grounded, and I contribute it to my spiritual well-being. I do not have the capacity or the energy to control every situation, but I can control my response.

2. I keep a positive outlook of my situation. Sometimes I repeat phrases throughout the day like, "I can make it," or I'll quote part of my favorite scripture, Philippians 4:13, "I can do all things." After saying this repeatedly, a few hours have gone past, and I've said these positive words many times. I am a firm believer that you will have what you say.

3. I change my actions. In order to get something new, you must do something that you have never done.

You Don't Have to Fear Failure

I'm so glad that I was not selected for the Bank of America Student Leader program the first time that I applied. After my application was denied, it motivated me to keep trying, evaluate myself, and discover some things about myself that I would have never known existed.

Before I applied again, I decided to update my resume and give the Bank of American Student Leader application another shot. The application for Bank of America was not solely based on work experience, but other factors as well. So, I made sure to review the essay questions that I had to answer, and I included recommendation letters. One was from the principal of my school and the other was from my teacher, Mrs. V, who told me about the Bank of America Stock Market Challenge. Obviously, it was impossible for me to include everything. A good rule of thumb is to keep your resume no more than two pages. It is actually better to have one page, if possible. This time, I included more volunteer experiences on my resume. I included my update resume below:

Isaiah Swift

Address • isaiahswift385@gmail.com • Phone Number

OBJECTIVE

Innovative professional with experience in customer service and sales seeking employment in related field. Highly motivated and self-starter, eager to work in a career where I can apply my skill set and knowledge.

WORK EXPERIENCE

Chick-Fil-A

March 2015 - Present   **Cashier / Host**   Norfolk, VA.

- Responsible for taking and giving out orders from the customers
- Required to balance cash drawers, answer questions from the customers with regards to the menu items and other special services offered by the restaurant
- Accompany guests to their seats in a very sociable manner while upholding the flow of customers arriving and leaving the restaurant
- Oblige to all the requirements of every customer especially those with disabilities
- Meet and exceed customers' total dining experience through customer service

Norfolk Emerging Leader Internship (NEL)

June 2015 - August 2015 (Seasonal)   **NEL Intern**   Norfolk, VA.

- Assisted in maintaining the overall cleanliness of the corporate office building
- Various tasks included landscaping, sweeping storage rooms for city of Norfolk equipment and needle-gunning machinery/painting machinery for city purposes
- One of 200 students selected from over 2000 applicants
- Selected as team leader for the summer

EDUCATION

Maury High School

Sept. 2012- June 2016   **Advanced Diploma**   Norfolk, VA

- National Honor Society 2013- Present
- President of DECA (Association of Marketing Students) 2014-Present
- FBLA (Future Business Leaders of America) 2014- Present
- Branch Manager of Commodore Branch 2015- Present
- Tidewater Community College Dual Enrollment Course
- Roc Solid Foundation 2015- Present

SKILLS

Word, Excel, PowerPoint, technical writing; advanced composition; video production; providing knowledge of word processing, Desktop Publisher and Web software.

REFERENCES

Available upon request.

I remember receiving the call that I got accepted into the Bank of America Student Leader program. I was ecstatic. A few months later, I began my internship experience working at the local YMCA in my community. I worked full time, and I received about $10 per hour working 35 hours a week, which wasn't bad for a summer internship. During this time, my schedule would not allow me to commit to Chick-Fil-A and the Bank of America Student Leader internship at the same time, so I decided to take the opportunity with Bank of America.

My job description at the YMCA included:

- Child watch- Interacting with children in summer camp programs for the YMCA

- Interactive zone- Providing assistance to youth using interactive fitness equipment

- Aquatics- Assist in swim lessons

- Membership- Assist front desk or administration staff

- Active older adults- Help implement activity

- Sports- Assist coaches and team members

- Development office- Assist development staff

- Attend and participate in weekly family center staff and annual giving campaign meetings

- Visit and observe a family center board meeting

- Meet each senior leadership team member and department staff- marketing, financial development, membership and leadership development

Lessons Learned during the Summit Week

As a part of the internship program, I attended a student leader summit in Washington D.C. with four other girls that were selected from my market as well. The best way to describe the five days that I was there was simply remarkable. Bank of America covered so many issues from personal development to leadership. I spent a week with over 200 student leaders from around the country who had different political backgrounds, religions and ethnicities. We all had the same energy to create a change in our local communities.

I remember a room full of excitement, when the student leaders competed in a social services simulation hosted by LIFTopolis. The CEO and co-founder of LIFT, Kirsten Lodal, took the stage to remind the students about the importance of having empathy. She discussed the challenges faced by many low-income families and how LIFT works to provide solutions. She explained that in order to have empathy, "you must put yourself in someone else's shoes." The simulation that students participated in consisted of student leaders receiving a new identity regarding their income, ethnicity, and career.

During the LIFTopolis, students were given about four, 10-minute "days" to visit social service providers and strategize how they would plan for the next day. It didn't take long for many of us to realize that this is what most of our parents have to deal with on a regular basis. Our job, based on the new identity we were given, was to secure childcare for our children and employment and housing for our families. We had to ask social services for help in doing so. Many of the social services would turn some of the students away. Following the mock simulation, Kristy connected out experiences during the LIFT's mission of how they are trying to reduce poverty in America.

Based on her presentation, it's easy to see how people can get trapped in this cycle of poverty. With basic services so difficult to obtain, you can quickly lose hope. However, many of the student leaders were able to come up with ideas on how we could create better solutions to the social service system. Two student leaders from each table presented their group's "big ideas" on stage. With enthusiasm, students outlined solutions including better training for customer service providers, enacting mandatory financial literacy courses in schools and even utilizing social media to bring social service systems into the digital age to promote awareness.

The student leaders also participated in an event called Mock Congress where we got to role play and experience first-hand what it's like to be a Congress person. Then, the following day, we traveled to Capitol Hill where each intern had the opportunity to meet their local congressman and congresswoman. We formed a close-knit group of people. About 15 student leaders were assigned the entire week to a workshop group. This workshop was a like my family for the week while I was in D.C. While getting to know other student leaders, I realized that everyone has a story. You shouldn't judge anyone on their outside appearance. Most people have a limited world view, me included. I sometimes have a hard time meeting and understanding people who do not dress like me, look like me or speak my language. Because there was so much diversity at the conference, I was able to expand my world view and get a broader perspective of American society.

Because the Bank of America Student Leader experience was great, I want you to hear about how this internship helped another great individual as well. I want to highlight another student leader that I had the opportunity to meet during my summer in Washington D.C. His name is Carlos Polanco. Carlos led a peaceful protest on the footsteps of the Lincoln Memorial where Dr. Martin Luther King Jr. gave his "I Have a Dream" speech. The student leaders made an appeal to Congress to work towards reducing gun violence. If you search on www.youtube.com, the video can be viewed when you type in, "2016 Bank of America Student Leaders Peaceful Protest."

I had the opportunity to be in this video and a part of history. I recently interviewed Carlos to catch up on his most recent work. He was very busy and provided me with a few minutes of his time to discuss his involvement with being selected as a National Youth of the Year for the Boys and Girls Club, where he represents nearly 4 million teens and won $145,000 in college scholarships.

CARLOS POLANCO

1. Who is Carlos Polanco?

He was born in the Dominican Republic. Carlos remembers waking up to wonder whether he had electricity before heading to school each morning. Carlos' family came to the United States when he was just 5-years-old. Learning English in the first grade, Carlos was constantly reminded of the importance of an education. He started coming to the Boys & Girls Club as a volunteer in the KinderCare program, where he discovered his passion for education.

Carlos prides himself not just on academic achievement, but also on his civic engagement. He helped found the Clifton Student Union, which is completely student-run, student-led and student-oriented, providing representation to Clifton's Education Committee. In this capacity, he's rewritten the school dress code, addressed the lack of AP classes and led a peaceful march of more than 350 students advocating for fair funding.

Carlos will be the first in his family to attend college this fall when he heads to Dartmouth College. His American dream is to become a Supreme Court Justice.

2. How did you get involved with the Bank of America Student Leaders program, and how would you best describe your internship experience?

I found the program searching online for internship opportunities. I applied and thankfully was accepted. My internship experience was great because I was able to learn the different things that are required to run a non-profit.

3. **Explain the process of being selected as a Boys and Girls Club National Youth of the Year?**

To become the NYOY, you start at the local level. I was nominated by my club and competed against 10 other candidates in my club. When I won my club, I was 1 out of 4,300 across the country who won their club nomination. I then submitted an application, which was evaluated at the state, regional, and national level. The application process consisted of three essays, three letters of recommendation, two supporting documents, volunteer history, work history, and academic record. I then had to deliver a 3-minute prepared speech and was interviewed by a panel of judges.

4. **Maybe there is student in high school who is reading my book right now and they feel that they are incapable of achieving their dreams because of their current circumstance. What three tips would you give that student to overcome doubt?**

Don't stop. You have to keep moving even if that means moving backwards. But keep moving until it's in the direction you want, and then work harder. I barely sleep because I'm always doing something. Be a global force for good.

5. **How can people stay connected with you?**

People can stay connected with me via Instagram @CPOLANCO18, Twitter @CPOLANCO18 or on linkedin in Carlos Polanco.

Chapter 7
Understand the Importance of
Financial Education

"The goal isn't to live forever; it's to create
something that will." ~Chuck Palahniuk

Earlier, I discussed the importance of beginning your work ethic at a young age. Let's face it, for some, balancing a job in high school can be very challenging during the school year or during the summer. You might discover that you have other interests, so let's dive into them. During the summer of my junior year, I worked three jobs and earned over $3000. I didn't mention that to brag, it was just the results of my actions. Three job opportunities were presented, and I had to create a schedule that best fit me.

My First Credit Card

As I mentioned earlier, my mother was a banker, and she emphasized the importance of having credit at an early age. For those of you reading this book, you might not have your own credit card yet, but understanding the concepts early on will help you in the future. Before banks give you a credit card, they like to see that you are employed, and most banks will ask you to verify how much income you make a month.

I knew that one of the first things that I wanted to do when I turned 18 was get my own credit card. Most adults will tell you to stay away from credit cards because they fear that you will use them carelessly and get into financial trouble.

Well, here's why I wanted a credit card:

- I wanted to establish credit history as early as possible.

- In high school, I used to manage the school credit union.

- Establishing credit early creates more long term economic opportunities.

- I set a goal to achieve a credit score of 700 and higher in one year.

- I wanted to maintain a great relationship with my credit union.

The first time that I applied for a credit card, my application was denied. This was simply because I did not have enough verifiable income to prove that I could responsibly manage a card, so I opened a savings and checking account with the bank that I was applying for a card. I continued to work hard on my job until I was receiving higher paychecks. I would set aside money each month to go to my savings account, and I continued this for about 6 months. When I reapplied after the six months, I was approved for my first secured credit card. I was able to begin the process of building my credit. When a lender pulls your credit score to see if you qualify for credit, it is known as a hard or soft inquiry.

Why do hard and soft inquiries matter?

A *hard inquiry* can occur when a bank or lender checks your credit before deciding whether to approve your application. This type of inquiry can stay on your credit reports for about two years.

Several hard inquiries on your reports could be a red flag for credit card companies. Too many hard inquiries could be a sign of a high-risk borrower who is opening a lot of accounts because they are low on cash and potentially about to get into a lot of hard-to-repay debt. Credit issuers generally shy away from giving credit to consumers who they think won't be able to pay back the debt.

A *soft inquiry* happens when a person or company checks your credit as part of a background check. For example, this can happen when a lender checks your credit without your permission to see if you qualify for certain credit card offers. After you graduate college, your potential employer might also run a soft inquiry before hiring you or a landlord might pull your credit before they decide to rent an apartment to you.

Unlike hard inquiries, soft inquiries won't affect your credit scores. (They may or may not be recorded in your credit reports, depending on the credit bureau.) The three credit bureaus are Transunion, Experian and Equifax.

How Does Credit Work?

A credit card is a loan from the bank that you have to pay back with interest. You can make purchases now and pay them at a later time. If you do not make your payment on time each month, then the bank will charge you interest, and it can cause your score to lower. People with good credit typically keep their credit utilization rate under 30% each month, which means if they have a limit of $300, then they don't spend no more than $90 each month. Practicing this habit will help you qualify for lower interest rates from the bank.

Secured v. Unsecured Credit Cards

- Most millennials qualify for a *secured credit card*. Lenders require you to put money down that is equal to your credit limit. So, let's say your limit is $150, then you would have to put down $150 on that card.

- *Unsecured cards* do not have a limit on them, and they are not secured by a collateral, which means it does not require you to put down a security deposit.

When you should apply for credit?

- If you are between the ages of 18 and 21, federal law requires that you have verifiable independent income to apply for a loan.

- If you are 18 and under and have no verifiable independent income, you can open a joint account with a parent as a cosigner. In this case, both your parent and you are liable for charges.

- Your parents can make you authorized users of their own accounts before you turn 18, but parents are liable for debt their children incur on these cards.

- Apply for a credit card when you feel that you are disciplined and responsible.

The Benefits of Owning a Credit Card

- You receive lower interest rates on cars and loans.

- You have a better chance to get approved for a loan.

- The bank will eventually give you higher credit limits.

- You qualify for lower car insurance rates.

What is a good score?

A credit score of 700 or above is considered good. A score of 800 or above on the same range is excellent. Higher scores represent better credit decisions and can make creditors more confident that you will repay your future debts as agreed.

What is an Asset and a Liability?

One of the first business books that I ever read was a book called *Rich Dad, Poor Dad* by Robert Kiyosaki. By purchasing his book and reading and applying the principles, you are making a great investment into your future. At the age of 13, I recall stumbling across this book at my uncle Mark's house. The title caught my attention, so I closed the bedroom door, sat on the floor and began reading.

Basically, this book explains the difference between an asset v. liability. An asset puts money into your pocket and a liability takes money out of your pocket. As you navigate your way through life, many of you will become homeowners. If you have a spare bedroom in your house and you decide to rent it out to a roommate, then your home becomes an asset. It becomes an asset when you have a positive cash flow after you deduct the rental income. If you purchase a home and you take on full responsibility of the mortgage, utilities, landscaping, maintenance, insurance, personal property taxes and interest, then your house is not an asset. It is a liability. Knowing these personal finance basics will help you make better purchase decisions after you graduate high school. The goal is to create more assets than liabilities.

Ways I invest in myself

- I believe in affirmations. What you say reflects who you are. The average human speaks 12,000 times a day. The difference between a successful person and an unsuccessful person is what they speak to themselves. Positive affirmations change the way you think, the way you speak, and ultimately, the way you view yourself.

- Instead of buying name brand items at the store and spending $200 on a pair of shoes, I shop at the local thrift stores or find deals on amazon. It takes discipline in the beginning, but you will eventually get used to it. Ultimately, my frugality increases my spending power.

- I consistently read business books on a weekly basis. I believe that reading is one of the ways to attain success. Books can give you ideas that you may have never thought of. Find a book that interests you. You can do this by researching a successful person that you look up to and see if they wrote a book.

- When you have free time in your car, after school, or while you are exercising, I highly recommend switching your music to a quick podcast. A few podcasts that I like listing to are, "The Side Hustle Show" by Nick Loper; "The Rise of the Young" by Casey Adams; and "Smart Passive Income" by Pat Flynn.

- Schedule an appointment with a business executive (with the permission of your parent or guardian). One time, I attended an event in my community called, "Heart of Ghent." I met a lady who was a financial advisor for Edward Jones. She was dressed down in regular clothes and was very friendly. After she talked to me for a while, she asked me if I would be interested in a potential internship program for Edward Jones during my junior year in college. This impacted me because at the time, I was a junior high school, so to think that she would take interest in me was remarkable.

    About a month later, I called her office and spoke with her assistant. The financial advisor was kind enough to allow me to come to her office and speak with her regarding the summer internship. She ended up speaking to a personal finance class at my high school regarding her role as a financial advisor and the benefits of working for Edward Jones. I was able to establish a relationship with a financial advisor before I even graduated high school and built a network with her.

Habits to avoid because it leads to a lack of financial education

- Watching long hours of TV

- Complaining instead of being positive

- Cater to everyone's opinion of you

- Spending time with bad influences (video games, peers)

- Overspending your credit card limit

- Eating a bunch of junk food on a daily basis (sodas, candy, processed foods)

Chapter 8
Take Advantage of Scholarships and Grants

"Quantity and persistence will get you the
outcomes you need." ~ James Altucher

Average student loan debt is rising to the highest it has ever been in decades. However, according to *Nerd Wallet*, roughly 45% of high school graduates do not take advantage of Federal Pell grants. Many students do not take advantage of these opportunities because they feel that it is time consuming and the application process is tedious.

According to the *College Board*, the average cost of tuition and fees for the school year is **$40,100** at private colleges, **$9,300** for in-state public colleges, and **$23,620** for out-of-state public universities. Most low-income households will have a difficult time coming up with this amount out-of-pocket, so they end up borrowing student loans to help cover the costs. Stop! Before you apply for student loans, why not explore the idea of scholarships?

5 things You Need to Know Before Applying for Scholarships

- The process can be tedious. There are nearly tens of thousands of scholarships available every year and it is impossible to attempt to apply for every scholarship, so:

  - Find your niche. What category best fits you?

  - Athletic scholarships, minority scholarships, academic scholarships, merit-based scholarships, local or national scholarships (there are hundreds of different types of scholarships)

- Have a scholarship team. My guidance counselor was one of the most supportive people that I knew at my high school. I actually remember her coming to my class one day to recommend a scholarship for me to apply for. Also, she would constantly send me scholarships that fit my criteria on a weekly basis. My grandma was beneficial in helping me apply for scholarships as well because when her church gave away scholarships, she would let me know. Local banks and credit bureaus provide scholarships, and when my peers came across these scholarship opportunities, they would share them with me.

  - Action to take: Develop a scholarship team that consists of parents, guidance counselors, peers and educators to be on the hunt for upcoming scholarships and deadlines.

- Apply for local scholarships because you have a higher chance of winning. Local organizations will most likely share scholarship opportunities with your high school. The best thing to do is reach out to your guidance counselor. Many of these organizations require that applicants live in the community for them to be considered for a scholarship.

- Use the same essays. Many organizations ask questions along the same lines such as, What are your career aspirations? How would receiving this monetary award benefit you? Explain more about the organizations you volunteer for? You can use this knowledge to your advantage and take previous essays that you've written and modify them for another scholarship application.

- Ask for recommendation letters. As a student, you should be prepared to ask at least 2-3 different individuals for a letter, whether they are an employer, teacher, mentor, coach or youth leader. Students should ask these individuals to provide strong, well-written recommendation letters that really provide value. Make sure to ask for recommendation letters within a reasonable time frame. I highly recommend at least 3-4 weeks before the scholarship application is due.

The Government can Provide Assistance

You can apply for grants and scholarships from the government by completing the <u>Free Application for Federal Student Aid (FAFSA)</u>. You should check with your guidance counselor to check the deadline for this application. These funds are usually awarded on the basis of financial need, and some states have certain academic requirements you must meet. Do these dollars go unclaimed? Definitely not. The only way this money is left on the table is if you don't apply so take advantage. Sometimes there are deadlines attached (especially for some states), so be sure to apply early.

How I won $108,000 in Scholarships and Grants

1. You need a planner to help you keep track of scholarships that you come across. On each scholarship, take a sticky note and write the deadline. One trick I used to do was, if a scholarship was due by the 20th of March, I would write the deadline for the scholarships at least 3 days earlier than the due date (excluding weekends). So, I would write the due date as Wednesday the 15th. That way, I would train my mind to submit all of my scholarships earlier than the due date.

2. I had fun with it. In high school, I applied for dozens of scholarships, especially during scholarship season, which is considered January – March. For me personally, applying for scholarships was like managing my own little part time job while I was in high school. Just like applying for a job, you have to sell yourself, know your brand, and have enough confidence to apply for money that is available because after all, this is an investment into your future. Have fun and enjoy the process.

    I would set goals on a weekly basis of how many scholarships that I wanted to apply for. I would mainly apply for scholarships that I found in the guidance office of my high school. My best advice to any senior in high school is to fall in love with your school's guidance office. Also, it was motivation for me to continue to apply for scholarships because my guidance office would email my scholarship application on my behalf to the scholarship committee. I was provided free official transcripts by my high school to include in my scholarship applications. You will not regret applying for scholarships, when you have to come out of pocket to pay for college.

3. Accumulate as many as you can. You do not need to have a high GPA or SAT score to apply for scholarships. I had a 3.6 GPA. My first scholarship I won was from a local credit union called Port Alliance Federal Credit Union. Actually, earlier in the chapter I stated that I worked as a branch manager for this credit union and obviously I banked with this institution. They offered a scholarship to high school juniors and seniors. I capitalized on this opportunity.

   If you don't know what you want to major in, still apply to that scholarship because you might be the only person that applied. Scholarship committees know that you might eventually change your major while in college, so they're not expecting you to have your life all planned out. You at least need to know what direction you want to go in after college. I knew that I wanted to major in finance while in college, but ultimately, I wanted to help others succeed by helping them create economic opportunities while leveraging my finance degree in the corporate arena. That's what scholarship committees like to read when reviewing applications.

4. Most scholarships require 5 things-

   1) Completed application

   2) Letter explaining your career aspiration, volunteer obligations, and reason for needing the scholarship.

   3) At least two letters of recommendation

4) A copy of your FAFSA form

5) Unofficial or Official Transcript

The requirements may vary but obviously, you can reuse this information and modify it accordingly. Accumulate as many scholarships as you can. I won the Port Alliance scholarship for $125 and it was my first scholarship. I remember my personal finance teacher stopping me in the hallway one day and she said, "Isaiah whatever you do, don't stop. If you keep applying, $100 will turn into $400, $400 will turn into $1600, $1600 into $6400." Some scholarships are renewable for four years.

The application takes literally 30 minutes to apply, so if you think about it, I allocated 30 minutes of my time to apply for a local scholarship, and I won. I just received $125 in a half hour. That's more than 17 times the cost of minimum wage at $7.25 per hour.

During my senior year, I applied for a second scholarship that Port Alliance offered to seniors that was $250, and I won. The goal is to accumulate as much as you can. The money adds up. In my essays, I added how I came from a single parent home, and I did not have a lot of money to pay for college. I stated not only how the scholarship would benefit me, but how I would go into the community and make a difference through volunteer service. Scholarship committees are willing to invest in you. In your essays, you have to be as transparent as possible. Try to include as much detail as possible regarding your career aspirations and what you would do to add value to the community once you obtain your degree.

5. I can't stress this enough. You must start local. National scholarships draw a lot of attention and therefore it is difficult to win those because they have so many applicants. This is not to discourage you from applying to national scholarships. If you find an opportunity that meets your criteria, then capitalize on it. However, local scholarships have limited requirements to apply, which will increase your chances of winning them. Also, the best way to find scholarships is to search www.scholarships.com. That website will provide scholarship information that varies by your state. Contact your guidance counselor and let them know that you are looking for scholarships to apply that meet your criteria, and they can find a scholarship to match a skill that you might have or you career interest. Also, peers can be a great source of contact for applying to scholarships. You never know where someone's parent might work, and their jobs are providing scholarships.

6. Pace yourself. The opportunities will come. I knew that I needed to come up with money to pay for college so my junior and senior years in high school were spent applying for local scholarships in my community. Between both years, I applied to more than 30 scholarships with the help of my mom, teachers, guidance counselors and mentors.

    One of my most memorable events was when I won a scholarship from an organization called the Gray Men's. The award was $1000. When I attended the scholarship reception to receive my award, it just so happened that the president of the university I had applied to was in attendance. When he saw that I and two other students were attending Norfolk State University as seniors straight out of high school, he walked up to the front of the stage in front of 900 and asked if he could speak to the MC. He whispered something to him. About 10 seconds later, the MC cleared his throat and said "I have an announcement to make. The president of Norfolk State University just said that he is going to double the scholarship amount for the students attending NSU!" I couldn't believe what I had just heard. The crowd roared and cheered. I went to the scholarship reception to receive a $1000 award and I walked out with $2000. I was so grateful for that opportunity.

7. If a college or university offers you a full ride, take it. I had many scholarship offers from other prestigious Ivy League schools, but I could not take advantage of their award money because I had declined to attend their institution. I didn't need their aid thanks to an award that was provided to me called the City of Norfolk Full Tuition Grant provided only to incoming freshmen at Norfolk State University. This award covered all my unmet needs. When I found out that I was selected to receive this award, I was shocked. Now, I could graduate without having to pay any federal or private student loans.

Chapter 9
It's all Worth it

Many students in high school limit themselves because they have a hard time becoming comfortable with being uncomfortable. They let limiting beliefs override their chances of being successful in life. In order to become successful in high school, you must first believe in yourself that it is possible. So much greatness is stored on the inside of you, and you have to maximize it. Don't hold it in.

In the beginning of the book, I talked about how I fell off of a bike and I related that experienced to how sometimes in life, many people might fail or experience setbacks. You might not literally ride a bike and fall off it, but in life, we make mistakes. In fact, many of you reading this book have made and are going to make more mistakes. The good news is that you can use those mistakes to fuel your energy so when you try again to tryout for the team, apply for a scholarship, take another test etc., you will be better prepared.

I mentioned that I was not born with a silver spoon in my mouth, so sometimes it was hard for me as a kid to look further into what life could possibly offer me. I would literally ask myself questions like, "Can I ever travel the world," "Can I ever be a millionaire," "Will I be able to solve a billion people problem," "What is something that I can provide to make life better for people?" As I look back, the decisions that I made in high school and a few of my, "falling off the bike moments" were actually seasons in my life that steered me in the right direction. My mistakes and triumphs are directing my life towards the answer to these questions. And for all of them, the answer is a resounding, "Yes!"

Start taking actions today that will lead you closer to your goals in life, and you will see results. Everyday we walk past opportunities. They are everywhere, but it only comes to those who make themselves available. You have to believe that you deserve every good thing that life has to offer. You are not a mistake. You are a part of a purpose.

When my mother was a single parent, I remember the day that she lost her job. I thought that she would be able to find another one soon, but that was not the case. Soon turned into later, but I knew that it was up to me to learn from that experience. So, I took advantage of internships, volunteer experiences and scholarships. You might be in a negative situation right know, but always remember that it is a blessing in disguise. You just can't see it yet. I realize that my actions in high school allowed me to go to college on a full ride scholarship, write a book, and meet thousands of people through my work experiences.

You will never maximize your potential if you are in your level of comfort. It just won't work. Following these steps that I give you will help you increase your list of networks in high school and ultimately beyond high school. Establish connections through volunteering, through social media and through job experiences.

In chapter 7, I talked about the value of financial education. Having a good credit history means that you have a great reputation, always remember that. Focus on ways that you can invest in yourself, so that when the time comes for you to offer your service to a company or provide your service to other individuals, you will be able to offer your best work. You must invest in yourself. Take time to read books, study a new language, invest in a passport, and create a video and upload to YouTube. You can use your knowledge to share with others and ultimately capitalize on it as well. This is how you can unlock your greatness.

The decisions that you make today will have a huge impact of where you land in five years. It's time for you to demand the best of yourself. If you find yourself in a negative situation and it seems that life is too much to handle, ask yourself this question "What have I done for someone else lately?" That simple thought can literally change your entire destination. It doesn't have to be something grand, but think about when was the last time you smiled at someone you walked past. Did you lend a pencil to someone that needed it? Maybe you can make an effort to open the door for a lady you see carrying a heavy load.

These are acts of kinds that can build your character. Start by doing something for someone else and in return, life will be good to you. Invest in opportunities. Don't avoid them. When you decide to take advantage of a good opportunity, not only does it impact you, but it impacts those that are around you. Reading this book will not fix every problem in your life. The decisions that you make after reading this book will change your life. It's up to you to take action. If you can't find an opportunity, create one. Take your negative circumstance, implement a new daily routine, embrace the process and watch the results. Trust me, it will all be worth it.

CPSIA information can be obtained
at www.ICGtesting.com
Printed in the USA
LVHW021750230120
644586LV00017BA/1695